A new source of income
In 24h.

Copyright

Formal education will make you earn a living. Self-education will make you a fortune." – Jim Rohn

"Investing in knowledge always yields the best interest." – Benjamin Franklin

"Lack of money is the root of all evil." – Mark Twain

"Once you have a solid base of knowledge, it becomes much easier to learn how to invest and handle money." – Rafael Seabra

"Money is a terrible master, but an excellent servant." – P.T. Barnum

This book was carefully created to help you discover and implement a new source of income in an amazing time: just 24 hours.

Yes, you read correctly!

In the world we live in, time is a valuable resource and the need to diversify our sources of income is increasingly evident, we seek quick and practical solutions to improve our financial situation.

It is in this context that the concept of*"a new source of income in 24 hours."*

This book aims to provide you with a comprehensive and actionable guide, filled with tried and true techniques, that will help you identify opportunities and implement a new source of income in such a short time frame.

The proposal here is to go beyond theory and offer a practical action plan, so that you can start generating results immediately.

From the conception of the idea to winning over the first customers, everything will be addressed in a direct, clear and easy-to-apply way.

This material is an invitation for you to immerse yourself in a financial transformation, putting into practice the necessary steps to reach a new reality in just 24 hours.

a brief introduction

Have you ever found yourself in a situation where a single source of income<u>Is it not enough to meet your needs and desires?</u>

Maybe you're tired of living on a shoestring budget, of relying solely on a job that doesn't give you the financial freedom you crave.

If you are looking for a radical change in your life, this material is the most valuable thing you can learn.

Right now, you're about to discover the secret of creating a new source of income in just 24 hours. Yes, you read correctly. This is not an empty promise or a magic formula. We are talking about a practical and effective method that can significantly transform your financial situation.

Understand that having a single source of income is like walking a tightrope without a safety net. At any moment, you can lose your balance and find yourself in a difficult situation. That's why it's crucial to diversify your income streams and ensure sound financial stability.

But why is it so important to have a new source of income? The answer is simple: security, freedom and opportunity. By creating a new source of income, you become less dependent on a single job or business. This means that even if something unexpected happens, like a layoff or an economic downturn, you will have other sources of income to fall back on.

Throughout this ebook, you will be guided step by step, module by module, towards building a solid and profitable new source of income. Get ready to discover innovative strategies, practical tips and valuable insights that will revolutionize your view of income generation.

The Various Baskets of Golden Eggs

Having more than one source of income is a powerful concept that involves diversifying your sources of financial gain, rather than relying exclusively on a single source.

Imagine yourself as a wise farmer who understands the importance of distributing your seeds in various fields.

Each field represents a harvest opportunity, a potential source of revenue.

Just as a farmer doesn't put all his eggs in one basket, it's critical to spread out your sources of income to reduce risk and increase financial stability. Each source of income represents a basket and each basket contains golden eggs, symbolizing the opportunities and gains that can be achieved.

When we only depend on a single source of income, we are putting our entire financial livelihood at risk. If something happens to that source, such as a job loss or a drop in business profits, our finances can be severely affected. However, by diversifying and having multiple sources of income, we create a safety net that protects us against the unexpected.

This offers you several advantages. First, it allows us to explore different areas of interest, talents and skills, potentially generating more satisfaction and personal fulfillment. In addition, it can increase your earning potential and provide greater financial stability, as income from different sources tends to offset any fluctuations.

Think of the different forms of income that can be developed: income from a job, passive income from investments, income from own business, property rentals, income from freelance activities, among others.

Each of these sources makes a unique contribution to our financial journey, bringing different benefits and opportunities.

Just as a farmer's fields are carefully cultivated and maintained, we must dedicate time and effort to nurturing and expanding our different sources of income. This can involve developing new skills, looking for investment opportunities, improving marketing strategies for one's own business, or building a diverse professional network.

However, it's important to remember that having multiple sources of income requires balance and effective time management. It is essential to find a rhythm that allows enough energy to be dedicated to each of the sources, without compromising quality or efficiency.

Consider this metaphor of the many baskets of golden eggs. Cultivate your fields wisely, distribute your seeds in different areas, explore diverse opportunities and watch your financial harvest expand. By having multiple sources of income, you are building for your financial future, strengthening your security and creating a path to profitability.

Choose to cultivate several baskets with golden eggs, and let financial multiplication be the catalyst for a life of abundance.

Developing a Mind
that outsources and automates

To achieve financial success and build multiple sources of income, it is crucial to develop a creative and entrepreneurial mindset.

A mind that is constantly looking for opportunities, innovative solutions and ways to expand its financial horizons.

One of the first steps to developing this mindset is letting go of the idea that you have to be the one to do everything.

It's natural to want control over every aspect of a venture, but confining yourself to that mindset can restrict your growth potential.

Instead, start thinking about how you can create systems, find people, or utilize tools that can do the work for you.

The mindset of delegation and automation is key to freeing up your time and energy, allowing you to focus on strategic tasks and pursuing new opportunities.

Ask yourself:

"Who can do this for me?"

or
"What tool or technology can help me automate this process?".

These questions will push you to look outside for solutions and to think beyond your own abilities and capabilities.

Now, you are an entrepreneur, an opportunity creator. Its role is not to perform all tasks, but rather to identify market needs, develop solutions and build a diversified financial ecosystem.

By letting go of the idea that everything has to be done for you, you free yourself to think at scale, leverage your resources, and find ways to maximize your earning potential.

This could mean hiring employees, outsourcing tasks, investing in technology or establishing strategic partnerships.

Innovation is a key element in creating new sources of income. Always stay on top of market trends, emerging needs and changes in consumer behavior. This information can inspire business ideas and open doors to new income opportunities.

A mind that creates new sources of income is willing to step out of the comfort zone, experiment and take calculated risks. She is open to learning from mistakes, adjusting strategies and persisting in the face of challenges.

So challenge yourself to think beyond your own abilities and skills. Free yourself from the idea that everything has to be done for you and start exploring alternative solutions.

Open your mind, think big!

The age of infoproducts

Knowledge has become a valuable asset.

If you have skills, expertise or experience in a certain area, selling infoproducts can be a highly profitable way to share your knowledge and turn it into a sustainable source of income.

But what are infoproducts anyway?

They are digital products that deliver knowledge and information in a structured and accessible way.

They can include ebooks, online courses, webinars, podcasts, videos and many other formats. The big advantage is that they can be created once and sold to an unlimited number of people, which means the profit potential is scalable and growing.

By selling infoproducts, you are taking advantage of the growing demand for online information and learning. People are increasingly interested in acquiring specific knowledge and skills to improve their personal and professional lives. That's where your expertise comes in and the opportunity to offer solutions through your infoproducts.

One of the great advantages of selling infoproducts is flexibility. You can choose a specific niche that you have deep knowledge and passion in, and create a product that meets the needs of that target audience. This allows you to work with what you really like and have expertise, increasing your chances of success.

The great thing about this market is that the sale of infoproducts offers the possibility of reaching a global audience.

With the internet, you are not limited to just selling to people in your locality. Your product can be accessed by people from anywhere in the world, significantly expanding your earning potential.

To succeed in selling infoproducts, it's important to take a strategic approach. This includes identifying your target audience, understanding their needs and creating a high-quality product that delivers real value. You will also need efficient digital marketing strategies to promote your infoproducts, reach your target audience and convert them into customers.

Create once and receive for years

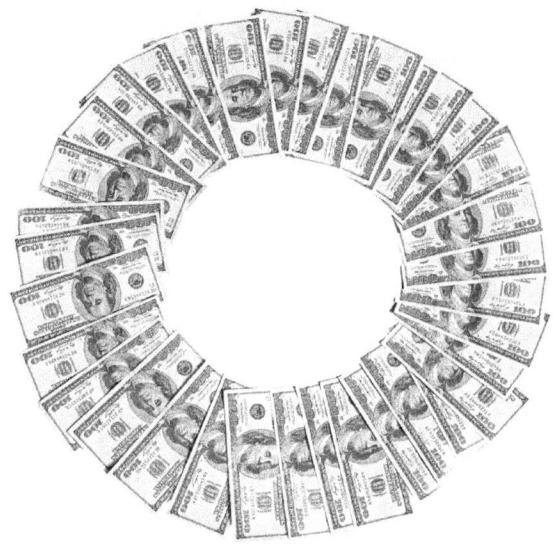

One of the great benefits of creating an infoproduct is the ability to generate earnings over a long period of time, possibly years.

Unlike other types of businesses or sources of income, where constant and continuous work is needed to keep the income flowing, a well-structured and planned infoproduct allows you to reap the fruits of your labor for an extended period, with a significant initial effort.

By creating an infoproduct, you are sharing your knowledge, expertise and experience in a format that can be easily consumed and accessed by your target audience.

Once you've completed creating the infoproduct, whether it's an ebook, an online course, a podcast, or any other form, you're making it available for sale or access.

From that moment on, your infoproduct becomes an asset that can generate recurring income.

Customers interested in your content will be able to purchase it or sign up for access to it, and you will be paid accordingly.

This income can be considered as passive earnings, since you don't need to make additional efforts for each sale or access.

The reason why you can make gains over a long period of time with an infoproduct lies in its digital nature and the possibility of automation.

Once the infoproduct has been created and made available, it is possible to set up automated systems for selling, delivering and accessing the content.

This means you don't need to be physically present for sales to take place, and the infoproduct can be automatically delivered to customers.

Also, a well-crafted infoproduct can be timeless. This means that your content remains relevant and valuable over time, regardless of changes in the marketplace.

Of course, in some cases, it will be necessary to carry out updates or additions to the infoproduct to keep it up to date, but, in general, the initial creation and structuring work will continue to generate positive results for a long time.

The longevity of earnings from an infoproduct is directly related to the quality of the content, its appeal to the target audience and its ability to solve problems or satisfy specific needs.

The more valuable and relevant your infoproduct is, the more likely people are to remain interested in it and willing to invest to acquire it.

Therefore, by creating a quality infoproduct, you are building a lasting asset that can generate earnings for an extended period, possibly years.

This provides an opportunity to build a stable and consistent source of income while you focus your efforts on new projects or expanding your business. Take advantage of creating an infoproduct once and enjoy the ongoing financial benefits it can provide over time.

Top 2 ways to sell infoproducts

There are two main ways to sell infoproducts and you can choose the one that best suits your profile and goals.

The first option is to sell your own knowledge, sharing your expertise and experience in a specific area. The second option is to sell other people's knowledge, acting as an affiliate or infoproduct reseller.

If you choose to sell your own knowledge, you are acknowledging the value and expertise you have in a particular subject.

You can create courses, ebooks, video tutorials or other infoproduct formats to teach and help others gain valuable skills and knowledge.

This approach allows you to share your unique passion, experiences and perspectives, creating an authentic and personalized product.

If you prefer to sell other people's knowledge, you become an intermediary, leveraging the expertise of other experts to offer high-quality products to your audience. As an affiliate or reseller, you promote and market third-party infoproducts, earning commissions for each sale made. This approach allows you to leverage other people's credibility and expertise without having to create your own products.

Both options have their advantages. By selling your own knowledge, you have the opportunity to build your personal brand, establish authority in your field and have complete control over the content you offer. On the other hand, when selling other people's knowledge, you can benefit from strategic partnerships, have access to products already validated by the market and save time and effort in the creation process.

It is important to highlight that we are all trainable beings and have the ability to acquire new knowledge and skills.

If you choose the option of selling other people's knowledge, you can dedicate yourself to learning about the product and its value proposition so that you can communicate with confidence and enthusiasm to potential buyers.

In this way, you become a facilitator, connecting people in search of knowledge with the solutions that meet their needs.

Whichever option you choose, remember that quality and delivering value are essential to success in selling infoproducts.

Focus on delivering relevant, well-structured, high-quality content that adds real value to people's lives.

Stay up-to-date in your area of expertise, constantly seek to learn and improve your skills to provide the best possible service.

Also remember that selling infoproducts is a continuous journey of learning and evolution.

Be open to experimenting, testing out different marketing strategies, listening to customer feedback, and adjusting your approach as needed.

With dedication, perseverance and a focus on providing value, you will be able to harness the unlimited potential that selling infoproducts offers as a sustainable and rewarding source of income.

The Infoproducer Market: An Infinite Opportunity to Undertake

Have you ever stopped to think about why selling infoproducts is one of the best options for starting a business?

The answer is simple: the market for knowledge and learning will never end.

It is a sector in constant growth and with an ever-present demand.

One of the advantages of entering this market is the low entry barrier. Unlike other businesses that require significant investments in infrastructure, inventory or physical production, infoproducts can be created and marketed with minimal costs.

All you need is your knowledge, a computer and internet access.

Another factor that makes the infoproduct market so attractive is the fact that we all seek to learn, from the beginning of our lives to the end of it.

The thirst for knowledge is an intrinsic characteristic of human nature. People are always looking for solutions, personal development, skill acquisition and overcoming challenges. And that's exactly what infoproducts offer: an opportunity to satisfy that demand and help other people achieve their goals.

We live in a digital age, where access to information is available anytime, anywhere.

Technology allows us to efficiently and scalably create and deliver content. With just a few clicks, you can create an online course, write an ebook or record a webinar and make it available to thousands of people around the world.

The sale of infoproducts is not limited to a specific niche. Opportunities exist in virtually every area of expertise, from business and finance to health, wellness, art, personal development and much more. If you have skills, experience or passion for a particular subject, there is an audience eager to learn from you.

Another advantage of this market is the possibility of building a recurring and scalable income.

Once you've created your infoproducts, they can be sold multiple times, without the need for physical inventory or production. This means that the earning potential is limitless, and you can build a passive income source where your initial work continues to generate profit over time.

It is important to emphasize that entering the infoproduct market requires dedication, commitment and a strategic look. You need to understand your target audience, identify their needs and create high-quality products that add real value. In addition, it is essential to invest in efficient digital marketing strategies to promote your infoproducts and reach your audience.

Therefore, if you are looking for a business opportunity with unlimited potential, selling info products is the right choice.

With a low start-up cost, growing demand and the ability to help people achieve their goals, you can embark on a promising entrepreneurial journey. There are no limits to the knowledge you can share and the results you can achieve in this ever-expanding market.

Unraveling the Secrets
of the Big Niches and Sub-Niches

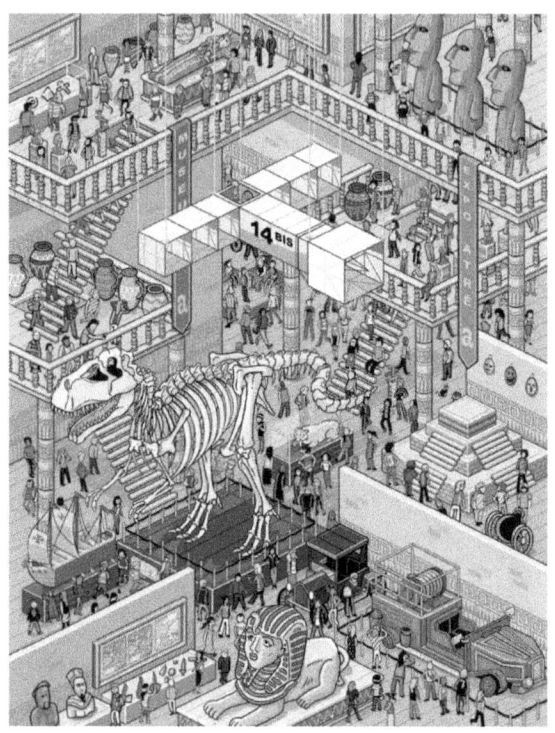

The niche is who defines the target audience of your business, allowing you to understand their specific needs, desires and problems.

As you delve deeper into the niche concept, you'll discover the existence of "big niches" and "sub-niches", strategies that can drive your success and maximize your results.

What is a niche? A niche is a specific market segment that has distinct characteristics and particular needs.

It is a specific group of people who share common interests, demographics, behavioral characteristics or problems.

For example, instead of targeting your business to "women", you could define a more specific niche, such as "women over 40 interested in fitness and wellness". The more specific the niche, the better you will be able to understand and meet the needs of your target audience.

Defining a niche is crucial as it allows you to become an expert in a particular market segment. By focusing your efforts on a specific niche, you can deepen your understanding of that audience's needs, wants, and pain points. This puts you in a unique position to deliver relevant and tailored solutions that specifically meet the demands of your target audience.

When exploring the niche concept, you will find two widely used strategies: the big niches and the sub niches.

Big niches are broad market segments that cover a wide range of people. They are characterized by having a wider and more general target audience.

For example, the "health and wellness" niche is a big niche, as it encompasses a wide variety of people interested in different aspects of health, such as healthy eating, physical exercise, stress management, among others.

Even though big niches offer a huge potential market, they are also highly competitive. It is necessary to create an efficient differentiation strategy to stand out among competitors and attract public attention.

This is where subniches come in. Subniches are more specific segments within a big niche. They focus on smaller groups of people who share more particular interests, needs, or problems.

For example, within the big niche "health and well-being", we can have sub-niches like "vegetarian diet for pregnant women" or "strength training for people over 50".

By specializing in a sub-niche, you become an expert in a specific field and can provide highly relevant solutions to that specific audience. Although the market is smaller compared to big niches, there is less competition and more likely to establish a deeper connection with your audience.

Defining the right niche for your business depends on several factors such as your skills, experience, passions and market demand. Here are some steps you can take to define the right niche for you:

Self-Assessment: Start by identifying your skills, knowledge, and experience. Ask yourself what your passions and areas of interest are. Consider your past professional experiences, hobbies, or any other expertise you have.

Market research: Conduct market research to identify trends, demands and needs of your target audience. Use tools like surveys, keyword analysis and social media platforms to better understand your audience's preferences and issues.

Identifying Potential Niches: Based on your self-assessment and market research, list some potential niches that match your skills and interests with your audience's needs and demands.

Competitor Assessment: Analyze the competition in each potential niche you have identified. See who the main players are, how they are meeting the needs of the public and identify opportunities for differentiation.

Niche Choice: Based on your self-assessment, market research, and competition assessment, choose the niche that most closely aligns with your skills, interests, and market potential. Make sure there is enough demand and opportunity to grow in your chosen niche.

Once you've defined your niche, it's time to dig deeper into knowing your target audience. Understanding your audience's needs, wants, pains and aspirations will allow you to create and deliver highly relevant products and content. Conduct research, talk to your audience, participate in communities related to your niche and always be aware of changes and developments within the segment.

In short, defining your niche is the path to success in the infoproduct market. Understanding big niches and sub-niches will allow you to identify market opportunities, position yourself as an expert and offer highly relevant solutions to your target audience. Remember that each niche has its own particularities and challenges, so be willing to learn, adjust your strategy as needed and always seek to improve your knowledge and connection with your audience. By doing so, you will be well on your way to building a successful business in the infoproduct market.

MethodSTRUCTURAL: Creating your Infoproduct from Scratch

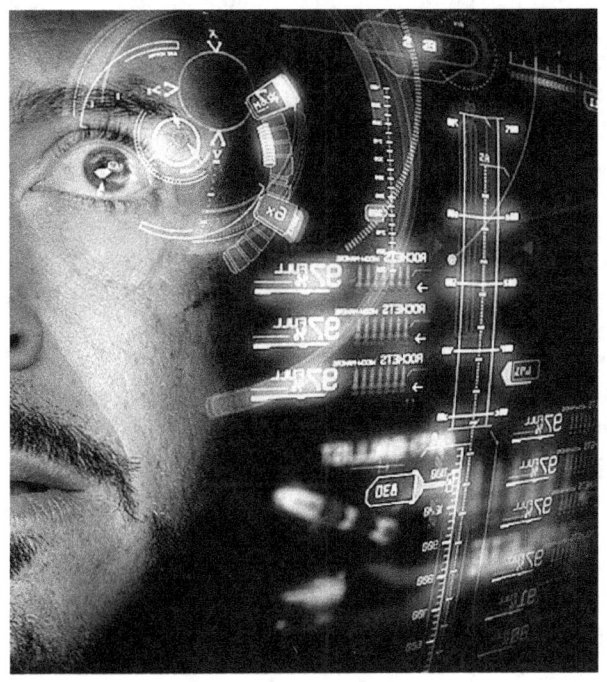

Imagine having in your hands a tested and proven method that will allow you to create high quality infoproducts, with a clear and engaging step-by-step process.

With the ESTRUTURALT Method, you will have access to the most efficient strategies to develop powerful content that impacts your audience and generates consumer desire.

E - Theme Choice: Start by selecting a relevant topic that is aligned with your knowledge and expertise. Consider your target audience's needs and interests when deciding on the subject of your infoproduct.

S - Audience Segmentation: Identify your target audience clearly and specifically. Understand their demographics, interests, wants, and issues. This will help tailor your infoproduct to meet the specific needs of that group.

T - Type of Infoproduct: Determine the format of your infoproduct. It can be an e-book, online course, podcast, webinar, video or any other format that is best suited to convey the knowledge you want to share.

R - Roadmap: Create a detailed roadmap for your infoproduct. Divide it into modules, chapters or steps, ensuring a logical and clear progression of the content. This will help organize your ideas and make the creation process easier.

U - Use Examples and Case Studies: To make your infoproduct more engaging and practical, include real examples and case studies that illustrate your concepts and show your application in real life. This will help your audience understand and apply knowledge more effectively.

T - Content Transmission: Choose the best way to transmit your knowledge. Use clear, didactic language adapted to your audience. Use visual aids, such as images, graphics or slides, to improve understanding and assimilation of the content.

U - Usability and Accessibility: Ensure that your infoproduct is easy to use and accessible to your audience. Check that the structure and formatting are adequate, that the technological resources are working correctly and that the content can be accessed on different devices.

R - Proofreading and Editing: Do a complete review of your infoproduct, checking for grammatical, cohesion, clarity and consistency errors. Consider hiring a professional to do the final editing, ensuring the quality of the final product.

A - Visual Attraction: Value the visual appearance of your infoproduct. Use attractive design elements, appropriate colors and a consistent visual identity. This will help convey professionalism and grab your audience's attention.

L - Launch and Promotion: Plan an efficient launch and promotion strategy. Use digital marketing channels, such as social networks, email marketing, strategic partnerships, paid ads, among others, to reach your target audience and promote your infoproduct.

T - Test and Feedback: After launch, seek feedback from your customers and make adjustments if necessary. Evaluate the performance of your infoproduct, check that the public's expectations are being met and always seek to improve the user experience.

through the methodSTRUCTURAL, you will have a practical and efficient guide to create your infoproduct from scratch.

Follow each step carefully, adapting them to your needs and your target audience. Remember that the quality of the content and the delivery of value are what will dictate the success of the business.

Artificial intelligence can help you by 70%

Artificial intelligence (GPT Chat) can generate content quickly and automatically, but the true essence, brilliance and authenticity often comes from the creative mind and human knowledge.

Human review is crucial to ensuring that content is correct, clear, engaging, and in line with the target audience's goals and expectations.

Artificial intelligence can help speed up the process of creating infoproducts, providing insights, suggestions and even generating pieces of content.

However, it is a person's attentive and critical eye that can spot errors, improve the text, add relevant examples, make the content more personalized and add that human touch that makes all the difference.

In addition, human review is also essential to ensure ethics and responsibility in the generated content.

Artificial intelligence can learn from large volumes of data, but it is the person who must make decisions and ensure that the content is accurate, unbiased and in line with appropriate values and norms.

Therefore, although artificial intelligence is a powerful and useful tool in the creation of infoproducts, the human presence is indispensable to guarantee the quality, authenticity and relevance of the content.

Collaboration between humans and technology is the way to create exceptional infoproducts that really add value and meet the needs of the public.

Nothing Is Created, Everything Is Copied: The Art of Modeling and Improving Existing Products

Have you ever heard the expression "nothing is created, everything is copied"?

Although it may seem contradictory at first glance, this phrase contains a powerful truth in the world of business and product creation.

The main idea behind this concept is that, instead of reinventing the wheel, we can be inspired by existing products and improve them, bringing innovations and adding value.

When we talk about copying, we are not referring to exact copying or plagiarism.

What we mean is that we can look at successful products and model them, adapting them to our own ideas and needs.

The secret is to develop the ability to question yourself:

"How can I improve this product that already exists?".

By observing and studying products that are already on the market, you can identify strengths and areas for improvement.

Analyze aspects such as design, features, user experience, customer service and marketing strategies. Ask yourself: *"How can I make this idea even more relevant, innovative and valuable to my target audience?"*.

This approach allows you to create products with much more assertiveness, since there is already an established base to guide your development. By modeling and improving an existing product, you benefit from work already done and leverage the learnings and insights that have emerged over time.

Remember that the objective is not simply to copy, but to add value and differentiation to the product. It is critical to bring your own perspective, creativity and knowledge to enhance what already exists. By doing this, you will be putting your brand and personal touch on the product, making it unique and attractive to your target audience.

When modeling existing products, make sure you are not violating laws or infringing on third party rights. Use the product as inspiration and a basis to improve your own creations, always respecting legal and ethical standards.

The art of modeling and improving existing products is a smart and effective strategy for entrepreneurs and infoproduct creators. By studying what is already available on the market and looking for ways to improve these products, you will have a solid foundation to create something new, innovative and in line with your audience's needs and desires.

So the next time you feel overwhelmed by the pressure of creating something brand new, remember: nothing is created, everything is copied. Look around, study, model and improve existing products. Bring your unique vision, your expertise and your passion to create something that exceeds your audience's expectations!

How to Create a Digital Ebook
with Artificial Intelligence in 15 Modules

Follow this step by step and watch the magic happen.

Module 1: Introduction

Presentation of the ebook and the author
Objectives and benefits of the ebook
Contextualization on the topic addressed

Module 2: Defining the Target Audience

Identification and detailed description of the target audience
Understanding the needs, wants and problems of the target audience
Importance of knowing the audience for the creation of the ebook

Module 3: Content Research

Conducting research and gathering relevant information on the topic of the ebook
Identification of reliable sources and references to support the content
Organization and structuring of the information obtained

Module 4: Ebook Structure Definition

Choosing a suitable structure for the ebook
Definition of chapters, sections and subsections of the ebook
Logical and sequential organization of content

Module 5: Title and Subtitle Creation

Development of an attractive and impactful title for the ebook
Creating subheadings that summarize the content of each section
Use of copywriting techniques to arouse the reader's interest

Module 6: Content Development

Writing the content of each chapter, section and subsection
Use of clear, concise and appropriate language for the target audience
Inclusion of examples, case studies and practical tips to enrich the content

Module 7: Review and Editing

Review of written content, correction of grammatical and spelling errors
Verification of text consistency and fluidity
Editing the content to make it more engaging and captivating

Module 8: Design and Layout

Creating an attractive and professional design for the ebook
Use of visual elements such as images, graphics and icons to enrich content
Ensuring proper layout, with spacing, fonts and harmonious colors

Module 9: Cover Creation

Development of an attractive cover that conveys the essence of the ebook
Use of images, colors and visual elements that relate to the content
Inclusion of the title and subtitle in a clear and legible way

Module 10: Formatting for Digital Ebook

Converting the ebook to a digital format such as PDF, EPUB or MOBI
Compatibility check for different devices and platforms
Ensuring proper formatting for reading on digital screens

Module 11: Adding Interactive Elements

Inclusion of hyperlinks to facilitate navigation in the ebook
Embedding videos, audios or animations relevant to the content
Adding interactive features that enrich the reader experience

Module 12: Final Review

Complete ebook review checking all elements, formatting and interactivity
Correction of any identified errors or problems
Guaranteed impeccable final quality

Module 13: Metadata Generation

Inclusion of relevant metadata such as title, author, keywords and description
Optimize for search engines and facilitate ebook discovery

Module 14: Publication and Distribution

Choosing the right distribution platforms for the ebook
Ebook upload on selected platforms
Definition of ebook dissemination and promotion strategies

Module 15: Monitoring and Continuous Improvement

Monitoring ebook performance such as number of downloads and reader feedback
Analysis of results and identification of opportunities for improvement
Periodic ebook update with new information and improvements

By following this step by step, using artificial intelligence as an auxiliary tool, you will be able to create a quality digital ebook, from initial research to publication and distribution. Remember to adapt each step to your needs and goals, always seeking to offer valuable and impactful content for your target audience.

MVP - The technique that will validate your infoproducts

The Concept of MVP (Minimum Viable Product) for Infoproducts

The MVP, or Minimum Viable Product, is a fundamental concept when it comes to creating and validating an infoproduct. It is an approach that allows you to develop an initial version of your product, containing only the essential elements, to meet the basic needs of your target audience. The main objective of the MVP is to test and validate the infoproduct idea with a minimum investment of time and resources.

When creating an infoproduct, many entrepreneurs make the mistake of investing a significant amount of time, energy and resources into a complete and finished product, without being sure that the market will receive it positively. This approach can be risky and lead to a waste of valuable resources.

It is in this context that the MVP becomes a smart strategy. By developing a simplified version of your infoproduct, you can launch it on the market more quickly and economically. The idea is to offer only the basic features and functionality you need to solve your target audience's problems or needs.

MVP is an iterative process, meaning you can launch an initial version and, based on user feedback, gradually improve and expand the infoproduct. This allows you to test market acceptance, validate your ideas, and make adjustments before investing time and resources in more complex features.

By opting for MVP, you can save time and money by avoiding developing unnecessary features or those that are not valued by your target audience. Plus, you get valuable feedback from users early on, which makes it possible to understand their needs, expectations, and preferences.

It's worth noting that MVP doesn't mean you're releasing a low-quality or incomplete product. Rather, the goal is to deliver a functional and useful product, but with a focus on essential functionality. Over time, you will be able to add additional features and improve the user experience based on the feedback you receive.

The MVP concept is especially relevant in the context of infoproducts, as they are usually based on knowledge and content. By creating an MVP for an infoproduct, you can offer valuable and relevant content, even if it is in a more simplified form initially.

In summary, the MVP is a strategic approach to create and validate infoproducts more efficiently. By developing an initial version that contains only the essentials to meet your target audience's needs, you can test and validate the idea with a minimal investment of time and resources. This allows you to save time, avoid waste and get valuable feedback to improve your product over time. Remember that MVP is an ongoing, iterative process, allowing you to grow and evolve your infoproduct based on your target audience's needs and preferences.

Conclusion

Creating an infoproduct is considered one of the best ways to generate a new source of income in a short period of time, even within 24 hours.

This statement is based on several factors that make infoproducts a viable and affordable option for entrepreneurs looking for quick results.

Next, I'll explain in detail the reasons why creating an infoproduct is an excellent opportunity to generate income in such a short period of time.

Low production cost:
Unlike physical products, which require investments in raw materials, production, inventory and logistics, infoproducts are created based on the producer's knowledge and expertise.

This means that the production cost is considerably lower, since it is not necessary to invest in physical materials or specific equipment.

With digital tools and resources currently available, such as editing software, content creation and hosting platforms, it is possible to create an infoproduct with little financial investment.

Time flexibility:
By creating an infoproduct, you have the freedom to set your own working hours and manage your time as per your needs.

This allows you to adapt to your current routine and create the product within 24 hours if you so desire.

Time flexibility is a significant benefit for anyone looking for a new source of income, as it allows you to reconcile the work of creating the infoproduct with other personal or professional responsibilities.

Scalability and global reach:
One of the great advantages of infoproducts is their scalability and global reach.

Once created, the infoproduct can be replicated and sold to an unlimited number of people, without the need for major additional efforts.

In addition, with the internet and digital platforms, it is possible to reach a global audience, regardless of their geographic location. This breadth of reach allows you to expand your sales opportunities and generate income in a short amount of time.

Demand for knowledge and learning:
The search for knowledge and learning is a constant in today's society.

People are always looking for solutions, personal improvement, professional skills and development in different areas.

Infoproducts offer exactly that: valuable, organized and structured content, able to meet the needs and demands of the public. By creating an infoproduct based on your knowledge or experience in a particular subject, you are offering something that the market is actively looking for.

Diversity of formats:
Infoproducts are not limited to a single format. You can create ebooks, online courses, recorded lectures, podcasts, webinars, and more.

This diversity of formats allows you to choose the one that best suits your communication style and the content you want to convey. In addition, this variety of formats also caters to audience preferences, offering different options for consuming the content you are making available.

Automation and passive earnings:
Once created and made available, the infoproduct can be automated, which means you can set up a system to deliver the product to customers in an automated way. This allows you to make passive earnings, that is, receive sales and generate income even when you are not actively involved in the process. Automation makes it possible for you to focus on other activities while the infoproduct continues to be sold.

In summary, creating an infoproduct offers a series of advantages that make it possible to generate a new source of income in a short period of time, such as 24 hours. With low production costs, time flexibility, scalability, demand for knowledge, diversity of formats, automation and passive earnings, infoproducts are a highly affordable and profitable option for entrepreneurs who want to start a new source of income quickly.

By using your knowledge and expertise to create an infoproduct, you will be offering value to the market and opening doors to opportunities for financial success.

Who is Matheus Martins Soares?

 Matheus is an Ex-Military / Presidential Agent, graduated in Marketing since 2018 and specialist in copywriting. He has written for more than 27 different niches, showing his ability to adapt to different topics and audiences. Throughout his career, he has worked in large companies, such as the largest business magazine in the country and the largest marketing consultancy in Brazil. Contributed to the success of important campaigns, generating + 30mm in sales for its customers. Published over 100 books on Amazon and gained readers in over 10 different countries. An expert in StoryTelling and UX Writing, he also works behind the scenes as a GhostWriter, giving voice to other people's ideas and stories. His method is capable of writing a book in less than 24 hours.

With a strategic vision and knowledge in marketing, he helps companies, authors and literary projects to achieve success. He found himself in the world of marketing, writing and human behavior, his ability to adapt to different challenges is a differential that makes him stand out in his field.